UNVEILING THE ART OF STRATEGIC GROWTH

Building Business Wealth Safely And Sustainably

Jimmy L. McIntosh

TABLE OF CONTENTS

INTRODUCTION

I have always wondered how to navigate through the business world in building unbreakable wealth and building a system for others to have a constant and permanent outflow of wealth in their businesses. I used to ask my mother questions about wealth creation. In the immense scene of trade and undertaking, the idea of business wealth remains an essential support point, encapsulating the pith of an association's monetary success and potential. Business abundance incorporates a broad exhibit of substantial and immaterial resources, mirroring the summit of an organization's endeavors, developments, and key choices. Any organization aiming to exponentially increase in wealth, having a lifetime income must build business wealth strategies. At its center, business wealth is an exhaustive proportion of the worth a business gathers after some time. It starts with unmistakable resources like actual properties, gear, and inventories, comprising the essential structure blocks of an organization's worth. Notwithstanding, the genuine profundity of business abundance grows a long way past the limits of material belongings. In this book, we dive into the subtleties of business wealth strategies, exploring the multi-layered aspects that portray it. From monetary measurements to vital preparation, from reasonable development to capable practices, we expect to unwind the privileged knowledge, wisdom, and insights that drive the creation, material, and upgrade of business wealth. Wonderfully enjoy reading.

CHAPTER 1

OUTSTANDING OPEN DOORS

Outstanding open doors speaks of the opportunities which keep emerging as long as the business is concerned. There would be immense and outstanding opportunities emerging for businesses and entrepreneurs. But the question I do, and I'm sure you do ask yourself is, How do we hold these open doors? These outstanding open doors gives entrepreneurs, organizations, and businesses access to the right key strategy to build wealth and achieve significant success. Critical or amazing opportunities for development, headway, or progress in different parts of life, like profession, training, self-awareness, or business venture. These open doors frequently present an opportunity to accomplish remarkable accomplishments, outperforming the customary and prompting significant advancement. They can emerge from unforeseen occasions, vital direction, organizing, jumping all over the perfect open door, or development. It's significant to perceive and gain by these opportunities to arrive at new levels and achieve striking objectives. These are the five(5) elementary open doors I have discovered in my journeyings in business wealth creation.

1. Technological Advancement And Innovation:

As an entrepreneur, an organization or a business, you need to look forward for technological advancements and innovations. Quick advancement in innovation and technology furnishes businesses, organizations, entrepreneurs with the potential opportunities to make creative items or administrations. Embracing arising advances like computerized reasoning, blockchain, or IoT can prompt troublesome plans of action and significant portion of the overall industry. I call this technology and innovative strategy.

2. Global Markets And Expansion:

I always tell my students that making it in the marketplace and building a firm wealth flow is understanding the global markets, their functionality in different spheres and its expansions. Globalization offers a huge likely market for items and administrations. As an entrepreneur, CEO, or business, you can quickly take advantage of the opportunity to extend your organizations universally, taking advantage of assorted buyer bases and driving dramatic development. I see this as an outstanding open door for businesses and entrepreneurs.

3. Investment And Financing Scene:

The accessibility of investment, private supporters, and crowdfunding stages offers new companies and developing organizations the kind of opportunities to get financing and fuel their growth and development. As a business and an entrepreneur, I believe you can try out their imaginative thoughts and plans of action to expected financial backers.

4. Coordinated Efforts and Organizations:

Coordinated efforts with different organizations or vital and strategic associations or partnerships can open doors for joint endeavors, shared assets, extended client bases, and admittance to new business sectors, eventually prompting expanded incomes and brand perceivability. This kind of open door or opportunity will determine how as an entrepreneur you function. Your partnership and coordinates must be strategically established as this can either accelerate your business growth or decelerate the growth of your business.

5. Broadening and Consolidation/Securing Open doors:

As a business and entrepreneur you can strategically investigate opportunities to differentiate your business portfolios or participate in consolidations and acquisitions. Vital expansion can alleviate dangers and entryways to new income streams. This will serve you as a brand that is firmly established.

As an entrepreneur and business you need to analyze and assess these opportunities in the context of your industry, business model, and target market to make informed decisions and capitalize on the most relevant ones for your business wealth and prosperity. I strongly believe this works for you.

CHAPTER 2

CLASSIC INTELLECTUALIZATION FOR REASONING

Every sector succeeds base on the kind intellectual standards they have built. Classic Intellectualization for reasoning is a central system that shapes how we see, examine, and pursue choices as well as making strategic decisions in different areas in the business world. Creating effective classic intellectualization is essential for key reasoning, critical thinking, and at last accomplishing wealth and abundance in business. In this section, we will investigate different mental models that can upgrade decisive reasoning and dynamic chasing business achievement.

1. **Understanding The Pareto Principle(80/20 Rule):**

   The pareto principle has been one of my favorite standards or classics in the business world as a visionary. The Pareto Principle suggests that approximately 80% of effects come from 20% of causes. In business, this means that a significant portion of outcomes often stem from a smaller set of activities or inputs. Understanding and identifying this vital 20% can lead to more focused efforts and increased productivity. This principle can help you as an entrepreneur or business to strategically position yourself for an outstanding wealth flow.

2. First Principles Thinking:

Reasoning from first principles is very essential. The first principles thinking is the act of scrutinizing each suspicion you assume you are familiar a given issue, then, at that point, making new arrangements without any preparation. It's one of the strategic ways to unlock creative solutions to complicated and complex problems. By understanding the core elements of a problem, As business leader you can innovate and build solutions from the ground up, enabling creative and original approaches. This classic Intellectualization improves your brand and assures potential build-up for an exponential wealth flow.

3. System Thinking:

Systems are everywhere. What makes a place effective is the kind of system built in that area. You need to understand that everything works and functions according to a particular system. Individuals are at the core of each and every mind boggling human framework or system - however they're frequently the most neglected. Effective and active problem solvers today know how to picture the bigger elements of the framework or system while remaining grounded in the necessities of individuals. System thinking sees an organization or businesses an interconnected arrangement of different parts and cycles. This model supports understanding what changes in a single piece of the system can mean for the whole business, encouraging all encompassing navigation.

4. Game Theory:

Game Theory is a hypothetical structure for conceiving social circumstances among contending players. In certain regards, game theory is the study of technique, or possibly the ideal decision-production of free and contending entertainers in an essential and strategic setting. The focal point of game theory is the game, which fills in as a model of an intelligent circumstance among levelheaded players. The way to game theory is that one player's result is dependent upon the methodology executed by the other player. The game recognizes the players' personalities, inclinations, and accessible methodologies, strategies, and what these systems mean for the result. Contingent upon the model, different prerequisites or presumptions might be important. Game theory has many applications, including brain research, transformative science, war, governmental issues, financial matters, and business. In spite of its many advances, game theory is as yet a youthful and creating science. Applying this model as a business holder, entrepreneur and an organization in business predicts results and plan by figuring out the activities and responses of contenders and partners.This classic Intellectualization will help you as an organization, businesses, and an entrepreneur to be relevant in the business world. Your relevancy determines your wealth inflows.

5. Innovation Ambition Matrix:

This matrix sorts thoughts in view of their oddity and possibility, directing organizations to seek after innovative undertakings that line up with their objectives and abilities.The Innovation Ambition Matrix centers around three unique classifications to characterize thoughts or developments. These classes are "CORE," "ADJACENT," and "TRANSFORMATIONAL." On every hub, there are three touchpoints: existing, arising, and new. These allude to the general acknowledgement or execution contrasted with the serious market. On every hub, these factors allude to "where to play" on the Y (markets, clients) and "how to win" on the X (items, resources).

● THE CORE INNOVATION:

The core innovation portrays limited scope advancement zeroing in essentially on working on the current item/administration without wandering into a neglected area. This doesn't mean duplicating everything from the opposition however it generally investigates advancing current contributions and adding some market standard highlights. A few choices here (for an item) could be configuration changes, online design, or straightforward feature.

● **THE ADJACENT INNOVATION**:

In the adjacent level, these innovations could require additional leg work, they as a rule expand on some current item/administration and can in some cases be found somewhere else. These innovations aren't be guaranteed to pristine however will without a doubt be new to your business. Given the factors on the X and Y tomahawks, these developments will either relate the current item to another client base or another item to the current client base.

* **THE TRANSFORMATIONAL INNOVATION:**

These innovations are appropriately named as they're groundbreaking to your business or the market at large. These ought to be things that aren't seen somewhere else on the lookout and are fresh out of the plastic new to your business. When done accurately, these developments can surface an altogether new market for your business to venture into. As a business you need to understand that tere will be a given measure of time and exertion devoted to groundbreaking development, you can further develop your center contribution without the group feeling like they're dismissing genuine, effective advancement in this level of the matrix.

Incorporating these classic Intellectualization into strategic policies engages you as a business entrepreneur and business pioneer to think basically, adjust to evolving scenes, and upgrade dynamic cycles. By getting it and utilizing these models actually, people as you, my dear reader, can upgrade your capacity to explore the mind boggling universe of business and accomplish enduring riches.

CHAPTER 3

UNDERSTANDING RISK IN BUSINESS

Understanding risk in business is crucial for effective decision-making and sustainable growth. For the purpose of this book, we will look into the types risks, strategies in handling each of the types and finally assessing risk tolerance. Risk in business alludes to the chance of experiencing adverse occasions or results that can frustrate an organization's capacity to accomplish its targets and objectives. These occasions can prompt monetary misfortune, harm to notoriety, functional interruptions, or lawful issues. Basically, risk addresses vulnerability in business, emerging from different interior and outer variables that can influence the association's presentation and supportability.

Understanding and overseeing risk is a principal part of maintaining an effective business. It implies distinguishing possible dangers, evaluating their probability and effect, and carrying out methodologies to actually relieve or oversee them. Risk is a daily matter in the business world. Let's look at the types of risk in business and the various strategies to handle each of these risks.

TYPES OF RISK IN BUSINESS

● MARKET RISK:

This includes variances in economic situations, like changes sought after, contest, or financial shakiness, influencing deals and income.

STRATEGIES:

● Expansion: Expansion in the sense that as an entrepreneur, you need to spread investment and item/administration contributions across various business sectors or fragments to limit the effect of unfriendly circumstances in a particular region.

● Statistical Surveying: As a business leader, entrepreneur or an organization, you need to lead intensive statistical surveying to grasp shopper inclinations, arising patterns, and serious scenes to pursue informed business choices.

● FINANCIAL RISK:

As a business holder and entrepreneur connects with monetary instruments and exchanges that might bring about monetary misfortune because of market unpredictability, financing costs, or credit.

STRATEGIES:

● Strategic Hedging: There must be a utilization of monetary instruments like subsidiaries to alleviate the effect of cost vacillations in products, monetary forms, or loan fees.

• Capital Administration: As an entrepreneur or business leader, it's of importance to keep a sound capital construction, streamlining the blend of obligation and value to diminish monetary gamble and guarantee satisfactory liquidity.

• **REPUTATIONAL RISK**

STRATEGIES:

• Emergency Correspondence Plans: Create and execute techniques to oversee correspondence during an emergency really, keeping up with straightforwardness and validity with partners as an entrepreneur, business leader, an organization.

• Moral Practices: areas of strength for maintain guidelines and social obligation to construct and save a positive reputation in the long haul. This strategy builds an entrepreneur for whatever comes up. Your reputation is an asset to your wealth inflows.

• ADMINISTRATIVE AND CONSISTENT RISK

STRATEGIES:

• Standard Consistency Reviews: You need to strategically lead incessant interior reviews to guarantee adherence to changing guidelines and consistency necessities.

• Legitimate Warning: The kind of association can determine your ability to handle risk and navigate through the risk for success. As a business, you need to team up with legitimate specialists to remain informed about administrative changes and guarantee consistency with regulations and industry guidelines.

These strategies, when customized to fit a business' particular conditions and joined with a proactive way to deal with risk the executives, can fundamentally upgrade an organization's capacity to deal with different sorts of dangers and support long haul achievement.

ASSESSING RISK TOLERANCE

Assessing risk Tolerance with regards to business wealth is a significant part of monetary preparation and vital navigation. Risk resistance alludes to an individual or association's eagerness and capacity to get through vulnerability or expected misfortunes in quest for monetary profits. Understanding and assessing risk resistance is fundamental for building an even speculation portfolio and pursuing informed business decisions. The most vital phase in assessing risk tolerance is characterizing clear monetary objectives and deciding the speculation skyline. Transient objectives might require a more safe methodology, while long haul objectives might allow a more elevated level of chance. There is that which is called risk capacity. Risk capacity the monetary capacity to retain misfortunes without essentially influencing the capacity to meet monetary objectives. It relies upon the ongoing monetary circumstance, income, obligation levels, and other monetary responsibilities. However, as an entrepreneur you need to understand that risk tolerance isn't static and can change over the long run because of different life altering situations or changes in monetary conditions. It's vital to occasionally survey risk resilience and change speculations as needs be.

Envision a tech startup, XYZ Developments, in its beginning phases with restricted capital. The pioneers have aggressive development designs yet know about the intrinsic dangers related with the profoundly serious tech industry. They need to painstakingly survey their gamble resistance to pursue informed choices with respect to speculation and extension. Assessing risk tolerance in business wealth implies a careful assessment of monetary objectives, ability to endure misfortunes, mental elements, and the utilization of fitting devices. A powerful cycle requires intermittent survey and acclimations to guarantee that venture procedures line up with the degree of chance an individual or association is willing and ready to bear.

CHAPTER 4

STRATEGIES FOR RISK RELIEF

In this chapter we will be looking into what I called "the advanced strategies for risk relief or mitigation." Your ability to mitigate risk helps you to navigate through the business world onto the acme of unfathomable successes. As I stated in the previous chapter, risk is a daily matter. It's path of the business reality. However, there is always a way to handle a matter. Risk Relief, implies distinguishing possible dangers and making moves to limit their effect or probability of event. Executing progressed systems or strategies for risk relief implies a diverse methodology pointed toward recognizing, evaluating, relieving, and overseeing gambles in a proactive and powerful way. Here is an itemized breakdown of cutting edge systems for risk help. These are nine (9) strategies for risk relief.

1. Risk Evaluation And Analysis

Direct a thorough gamble evaluation to recognize possible risks and their expected effect on the organization.

Use progressed risk investigation strategies like quantitative gamble examination, situation examination, and Monte Carlo recreations to evaluate the probability and seriousness of dangers.

2. Risk Mitigation Strategies

Create and execute risk mitigation techniques custom fitted to explicit risk recognized during the assessment.

Use a blend of risk mitigation strategies, for example, risk move (e.g., protection), risk evasion, risk decrease, and chance acknowledgment to oversee various kinds of risks you encounter as a business, an entrepreneur or an organization.

3. **Stress Testing And Scenario Plannings**

You need to direct stress tests and scenario planning to recreate outrageous occasions and evaluate the flexibility of the association's frameworks, cycles, and systems to endure these situations.

Assess how different gamble elements might interface during unfriendly circumstances and change risk the executives techniques in like manner.

4. **Utilization of Innovation and Investigation**

Utilize trend setting innovations like artificial intelligence(AI), Machine learning, and large information investigation or analytics to improve risk displaying, expectation, and dynamic cycles. Influence information examination to recognize examples and patterns in chances, empowering ideal and information driven reactions.

5. Business Coherence and Catastrophe Recuperation Planning

Foster hearty business progression and calamity recuperation intends to guarantee the association can keep up with basic tasks and recuperate rapidly in case of a troublesome episode.
Lead standard drills and reenactments to approve the adequacy of these plans and make vital changes.

6. Administrative Consistence and Legitimate Measures

Remain refreshed on administrative prerequisites pertinent to the business and guarantee consistence with appropriate regulations and guidelines.
Connect with legitimate guides to comprehend likely lawful risks and execute measures to actually alleviate them.

7. Cross-Practical Cooperation

Encourage cooperation effort and correspondence between various divisions and groups inside the association to guarantee a comprehensive way to deal with risk the executives.
Empower a culture of risks mindfulness and proactive revealing of likely dangers at all levels of the association.

8. Checking and Announcing Strategy

Carry out cutting edge observing frameworks or systems to follow risks continuously and get convenient alarms when risks surpass predefined limits.

Create standard and extensive risks reports for the board and partners, giving bits of knowledge into the ongoing gamble scene and the adequacy of chance administration systems.

9. Consistent Improvement and Learning

Lay out a culture of persistent improvement by consistently inspecting and refining risk the board processes in light of illustrations gained from previous encounters and arising best practices.

Put resources into preparing and improvement projects to upgrade the gamble the board abilities and information on workers at all levels.

Carrying out these high level or advanced methodologies or strategies for risk relief will assist you, my dear reader, with being stronger and versatile despite vulnerabilities and difficulties, eventually shielding their inclinations and guaranteeing supportable development. You're capacitated.

CHAPTER 5

STRATEGIC TRACKING OF TARGETS TO DISCOVER

In the journey for business wealth, strategic tracking of potential targets is a basic move toward recognize opportunities for development, extension, and productivity. Proactively observing the market and patterns empowers you to remain ahead, recognize promising possibilities, and go with informed choices. This chapter centers around an exhaustive aide for decisively following focuses to find business wealth. I will be unraveling eleven strategic tracking of targets to discover business wealth. These eleven strategic tracking has helped me on many occasions throughout my business journeys.

1. Understanding Business Wealth Goals

One essential thing to do as a business holder, entrepreneur or an organization is to muscle your understanding concerning what business wealth goals are. Understanding is the key to facilitating the process, progressing, and success of a work or project. Start by laying out clear business wealth objectives and goals. This could be extending a piece of the pie, expanding income, enhancing item contributions, or entering new business sectors. Adjust your following endeavors to these targets to guarantee pertinence and adequacy. Setting objectives and goals gives you an elucidating path on how to unlock wealth in your business.

2. Market Segmentation And Investigation

Having a clear understanding of your business wealth goals, your focus now needs to be on the market. Divide the market into segments based on relevant criteria such as demographics, geography, industry, or consumer behavior. Analyze each segment's potential for growth, competition, and demand trends. Understanding these segments helps in targeting specific areas for tracking.

3. Recognizing Key Pointers

Decide the key exhibition pointers (KPIs) that line up with your business goals and market sections. These could incorporate variables like client procurement cost, client lifetime esteem, piece of the pie development, or item reception rates. Lay out measurements to reliably gauge achievement and track them.

4. Competitor Analysis

With your firm understanding and knowledge, lead an intensive analysis of your rivals, both immediate and backhanded. Track their systems, item improvements, advertising drives, and market situating. Understanding competitor developments can feature holes and potential open doors on the lookout for your business to take advantage of.

5. Market Pattern Observation

Remain refreshed on market patterns, trends, customer inclinations, mechanical headways, and administrative changes. Use industry reports, distributions, statistical surveying, and online stages to stay informed concerning advancements that could impact your business possibilities. Also understand your established pattern of your business.

6. Systems administration and Industry Association

Draw in with industry affiliations, go to meetings, online courses, and systems administration occasions. Interface with experts, thought pioneers, and expected accomplices to acquire experiences into arising open doors, creative plans of action, and possible targets.

7. Using Innovation, Technology and Instruments

As a business, Influence progressed technological instruments like data analytics, machine learning, and AI to upgrade your tracking capacities. Use programming stages that give constant market insight, track industry news, and proposition cutthroat examination.

8. Laying Out Tracking Protocols

Foster organized protocols for tracking potential targets, incorporating explicit rules, edges, and timetables. Characterize boundaries like income limits, geological development, or innovative abilities to channel and focus on expected targets.

9. Regular Audit And Transformation

Constantly audit and adjust your tracking strategies in view of the outcomes and advancing economic situations. Be nimble in changing your center regions, measures, and following approaches to guarantee they stay lined up with your business objectives.

10. Cooperative Direction

This include key partners, stakeholders, and leaders inside your association to assess potential targets all things considered. Urge coordinated effort to guarantee a complete evaluation and determination of focuses on that line up with the organization's general technique.

11. Tracking Achievements And Learning

Measure the success of your tracking efforts by evaluating the acquisition outcomes and comparing them to the initially defined KPIs. Analyze the successes and failures to learn from experiences and enhance future tracking strategies.

In conclusion, Strategic tracking of potential targets is an essential part of finding business wealth. By utilizing an essential, information driven approach and adjusting to showcase elements, you can really uncover opportunities that line up with your business objectives and prepare to supported development and great success.

CHAPTER 6

STRATEGIC FINANCIAL PLANNING

Financial planning is highly essential in different sectors of life. In the context of business, Strategic financial planning assists organizations with remaining focused — and know whether they're going in the correct course. Strategic financial planning is a far reaching approach that includes figuring out, executing, and observing monetary systems and activities to accomplish an association's drawn out objectives and goals. It's tied in with adjusting monetary choices to the more extensive vital bearing of the organization. This arranging system involves an exhaustive examination of the association's monetary scene, current and potential future economic situations, and inward capacities. This planning incorporates different components, including budgeting, estimating, risk the board, venture arranging, and capital construction enhancement. In this chapter I will be sharing with you on ten steps to make a strategic financial planning.

1. Setting Financial Goals

The first step is setting financial goals. This is an essential step to strategically plan concerning your financial life. They make it more straightforward for you to make forfeits or adhere to a financial plan since you understand what result you're taking a stab at. They assist you with remaining fixed on the long haul. Inspiration - monetary objectives give motivation and energy and assist you with remaining restrained in your speculation cycle. Lay out clear and quantifiable financial goals, adjusting them to the association's general mission and vision. These goals ought to be explicit, attainable, sensible, and time-bound (Savvy).

2. Budgeting And Anticipating

Budgeting and anticipating are are a huge piece of an organization's capacity to set KPIs, short and long haul goals and pursue informed choices. The spending plan is basically a guide for where an organization needs to go, the costs they'll cause and income they'll procure. Foster a point by point spending plan that layouts anticipated incomes, costs, and ventures. Precise gauging in view of authentic information and market patterns is vital for settling on informed financial choices.

3. Risk Assessment And Management

Risk assessment and management are vital parts of financial planning, assuming a basic part in guaranteeing the drawn out progress and soundness of an association. Recognize likely risk and vulnerabilities that could affect the financial strength of your business. Foster procedures to relieve these risks, guaranteeing monetary strength and flexibility despite challenges.

4. Investment Planning

Investment planning is vital to accomplish independence from the rat race. It will assist you with creating pay, spending plan expenses, and limit charge. In addition, venture arranging likewise guarantees monetary security and wellbeing for yourself as well as your loved ones. Survey investment valuable opportunities and techniques to enhance returns while considering the association's gamble resistance and liquidity needs. Broadening and cautious resource designation are key standards in this part of financial planning.

5. Cash Flow Management

Viable cash flow management can increment benefit by decreasing the expense of getting and working on the profit from the venture. Keep a solid cash flow, momentary commitments, take care of obligations, and asset day to day tasks. Productive income the board includes observing money inflows and surges to guarantee ideal liquidity.

6. Tax Planning

Tax planning includes utilizing lawful procedures to limit charge responsibility and boost returns. Viable expense arranging can assist people and organizations with setting aside cash, increment income, and accomplish monetary targets. Strategically plan for tax suggestions by advancing assessment allowances, credits, and exceptions inside the lawful structure. Guarantee consistency with charge guidelines.

7. Debt Management And Capital Design

Assess the ideal blend of debt and value to finance your business development and activities. Adjusting debt to value proportions and understanding the expense of capital are essential parts of capital design arranging. As a business leader, entrepreneur, and an organization, The goal of an debt management plan is to utilize these systems to assist you with bringing down your ongoing debt and push toward killing it.

8. Financial Execution Monitoring

You need to understand that your business financial execution informs financial backers(investors) concerning its general prosperity. It's a depiction of its financial wellbeing and the work its administration is doing — giving knowledge into what's to come: whether its tasks and benefits are on target to develop and the viewpoint for its stock. Consistently survey financial execution against put forth objectives and targets. Break down budget reports and key execution markers to distinguish regions for development and course remedies.

9. Adaptability and Flexibility

We are many times informed that financial achievement is just a result of mathematical expertise and figuring out complex speculation methodologies. Be that as it may, Morgan Housel, in his generally acclaimed book "The Physiology of Money", challenges this famous idea. As per him, the fundamental part of financial achievement isn't the way savvy you are nevertheless the way in which you act. Your financial way, still up in the air by your own encounters, convictions, and predispositions, at last shapes your financial results. It is necessary as a business to perceive the powerful idea of financial business sectors and business conditions. Be prepared to change the financial arrangement depending on the situation to remain lined up with changing conditions and objectives.

10. Communication And Cooperation

Viable communication carries various advantages to financial planning. Further developed precision and nature of financial plans can result from clear communication and cooperation. More grounded client connections and trust can be worked through compelling correspondence, prompting expanded business and references. You need to have viable communication and cooperation among various offices and partners inside the association. Guaranteeing everybody is lined up with the financial objectives and strategies improves the probability of progress.

By integrating these parts presented to you in this book into an exhaustive vital financial arrangement, associations can successfully deal with their financial assets, relieve chances, accomplish their targets, and eventually flourish in a cutthroat market. I know your financial goal will be accomplished.

CHAPTER 7

INVESTMENT OPENINGS

An investment is a resource or thing that is completely intent on producing pay or appreciation. Appreciation alludes to an expansion in the worth of a resource over the long haul. At the point when a singular buys a decent as an enterprise, the purpose is not to consume the downside but rather to involve it in the future to make riches. An investment generally concerns the cost of some asset moment — time, exertion, cash, or a resource with at least some prospects of a further noteworthy result in the future than what was originally placed in. For the case, a fiscal backer might buy a plutocrat related resource now with the possibility that the resource will turn out profit latterly on or will latterly be vended at a more extravagant cost for a benefit. In this section, we will probe a multifariousness of investment openings accessible to people and associations trying to develop their riches and negotiate fiscal objects. Grasping different investment choices, their troubles, anticipated returns, and the general request patterns is a vector for going with informed enterprise choices.

1. Stock Market Investments

The term stock request alludes to many trades wherein portions of openly held associations are traded. similar fiscal exercises are directed through proper trades and by means of over-the-counter(OTC) marketable centres that work under a characterized set of guidelines.

Dealers in the fiscal exchange trade shares on at least one of the stock trades that are essential for the stock request. Under stock request investments, I'd love to talk about equities, Exchange- Traded finances(ETFs), and collective finances.

• Equities

Equity is shown yet to be a determined distance of an association. It's one of the crucial pointers that a fiscal backer proposes to distinguish an association's fiscal adequacy. In less delicate terms, value is the aggregate sum of cash that an investor is good to get on the off chance that an association's all's scores are paid off and its coffers changed. Examine investing into intimately traded businesses, emphasizing the eventuality for capital appreciation and profit pay. Make sense of the significance of probing associations, anatomizing financial summaries, and taking into account request patterns.

• Exchange- Traded finances(ETFs)

Finances that change on trades, by and large tracking a particular train. At the point when you invest into an ETF, you get a mound of coffers you can trade during request hours conceivably bringing down your threat and openness, while aiding with expanding your portfolio. You need to detail how ETFs offer diversified openness to different areas or resource classes, giving rigidity and chance administration to fiscal backers(investors). Talk about the benefits of low cost proportions and liquidity.

● **Collective Finances**

collective finances let you pool your cash with different investors to" mutually" purchase stocks, bonds, and different enterprises or investments.

They are controlled by complete cash directors who choose which protections to buy(stocks, bonds, and so forth) and when to vend them.
You get openness to every one of the interests in the asset and any pay they produce.
They offer a wide multifariousness of adventure methodologies, strategies, and styles. As a business leader and entrepreneur

you need to strategically explain the advantages of collective finances, which pool means from multitudinous fiscal backers to put coffers into a discerned arrangement of stocks, bonds, or different coffers. Examine colorful feathers of common means and their adventure price biographies.

2. Real Estate Investments

Real estate investments include the steal, the directors, and the deal or reimbursement of land for benefit. notoriety who effectively or latently invests into real estate is known as a real estate business visionary, an entrepreneur, or a real estate investor. Many fiscal backers effectively produce, ameliorate, or revamp parcels to get fresh cash- inflow from them. It's a notorious type of investment because of its true capacity for long haul returns and portfolio expansion or diversification under the Real Estate Investments we have:

• Residential Real Estate

Discuss investing in private properties for rental pay and likely appreciation according to your knowledge and experience. Cover points like property determination, property executives, and funding choices as business leaders based on your current knowledge and experiences.

• Commercial Real Estate

Commercial real estate is property utilized solely for business-related purposes or to give a work area instead of a living space, which would rather comprise private land. Most frequently, commercial real estate is rented to inhabitants to direct pay-creating exercises. This general class of land can incorporate everything from a solitary retail facade to a tremendous mall. Strategically explain the advantages and difficulties of putting resources into business properties like places of business, shopping malls, and modern edifices. Underscore renting procedures and market investigation.

Bonds And Fixed Income

Fixed income is a resource class that is a normally held investment since it helps save capital. Fixed-income investments, or bonds as they are regularly known, normally give a top-notch above expansion and experience less return unpredictability contrasted with shares. Fixed income is held for the consistent revenue stream the standard coupon installments give. Bonds can offer broadening benefits since they frequently act the other way to shares. Bond investment, consequently, helps to bring down the risk level inside a broadened portfolio. One way an administration or an organization can get the cash they need for their tasks or drives is to sell bonds.

All in all, a bond is a credit sold or given by the borrower(issuer) and bought by the lender(investor). We have Government Bonds and Corporate Bonds.

● **Government Bonds**

These are bonds given by a public government, designated in the nation's own cash, for instance, Australian Ward Government Bonds and US Depositories. Government securities are normally alluded to as hazard-free securities with shallow default risk and are among the most secure investments, in light of the fact that the public authority can increase government rates or print cash to reclaim the security at development. Bonds given by public state-run administrations in unfamiliar monetary standards are ordinarily alluded to as sovereign bonds. Discuss investing in officially sanctioned or government bonds, featuring their well-being and fixed-interest installments. Depict the kinds of government bonds, for example, depository bonds, and their part in a differentiated portfolio.

• Corporate Bonds

These are bonds given by associations to fund-raise for business purposes, for illustration, to grow tasks or asset new undertakings. Commercial securities, for the utmost part, pay advanced rates more than government securities since they will relatively frequently be more dangerous. Commercial bonds have a great numerous evaluations, mirroring the way that the fiscal strength of sponsors can change fundamentally. However, allude to the standing office member),(if it's not too important trouble High- return securities are given by lower- quality corporates and therefore have better returns to make up for the redundant dereliction threat. So, in this, clarify how commercial bonds are given by associations for raising capital and give ordinary interest inaugurations. Talk about credit scores, threat evaluation, and the security request rudiments. These are essential.

3. Alternative Investments

An indispensable investment is a fiscal resource that does not can be distributed as one of the traditional investment classes. Traditional groups incorporate stocks, bonds, and plutocrats. optional enterprises can incorporate nonpublic value or investment, collective finances, oversaw prospects, artificer, collectibles, wares, and inferior contracts. Real Estate is also constantly named an indispensable investment. Under indispensable investments, we've goods and cryptocurrency.

● **Commodities**

Commodity finances invest in natural substances or essential horticultural particulars, known as wares. These means put coffers into precious essence, like gold and tableware, energy means, like oil painting and petroleum gas, and agricultural wares, like wheat. Earthenware means may likewise put coffers into the associations that produce these products. thus, detailed investment into wares like gold, oil painting, and horticultural particulars. Talk about the job of particulars in broadening and supporting against expansion.

- **Cryptocurrency**

Cryptocurrency, then called cryptographic plutocrat or crypto, is any type of cash that exists precisely or for all intents and purposes and uses cryptography to get exchanges. Digital currencies do not have a focal paying or managing authority, rather exercising a decentralized frame to record exchanges and issue new units. Cryptocurrency is a motorized investiture frame that does not depend on banks to check exchanges. It's a distributed frame that can empower anybody anywhere to shoot and get inaugurations. Rather than being factual cash hefted around and traded in reality, cryptographic plutocrat inaugurations live absolutely as advanced passages to a web-grounded data set portraying unequivocal exchanges At the point when you move digital plutocrat reserves, the exchanges are kept in a public record. Cryptographic plutocrats are put down in motorized holdalls . Cryptocurrency accepted its name since it utilizes encryption to confirm exchanges. This implies that progressed rendering is associated with putting down and communicating cryptographic plutocrat information among holdalls and to public records. The point of encryption is to give security and well- being. The main Cryptocurrency was Bitcoin, which was established in 2009 and remains the most popular moment. A significant part of the interest in digital currencies is to change for a benefit, with observers on occasion driving costs overhead. As a business leader and an entrepreneur, explain the idea of digital currencies, their true capacity for significant yields, and the affiliated troubles. Stress the significance of ferocious disquisition and understand the unstable idea of the crypto request.

Work out strategically with the different investment openings talked about in this chapter, emphasizing the significance of expansion, threat appraisal, and conforming gambles to individual financial objects. I amp my dear peruser, to look for complete fiscal guidance prior to pursuing any investment choices.

CHAPTER 8

INNOVATIVE BUSINESS RESULTS

In this chapter, we dive into the groundbreaking force of Innovation inside the business domain. Development is a foundation for development, separation, and supportability in the present powerful market. We will investigate how organizations can cultivate a culture of development, saddle arising advances, and gain by imaginative procedures to accomplish unmistakable and theoretical outcomes.

Understanding Innovation In Business

Innovation in the business domain alludes to the creation, improvement, and use of groundbreaking thoughts, processes, items, administrations, or strategies that lead to critical upgrades in different parts of the business. It includes changing existing practices or acquainting novel methodologies with fulfilling developing business sector needs, improving effectiveness, or addressing difficulties.

Types Of Innovation

There are several types of innovation. Understanding the types of innovation as a business leader and entrepreneur can build you and prepare you in different sectors in the business world.

1. PRODUCT INNOVATION

Making new or further developed products, elements, or administrations to address client issues or wants. Product Innovation envelops creating and acquainting new or further developed items with meet shoppers' changing necessities and wants. It includes more than minor changes or adjustments; it rejuvenates new thoughts, pushes limits, and conveys notable arrangements that dazzle the market. Really ponder the conceivable outcomes that item advancement opens. From progressive advancements like self-driving vehicles and computer generated reality headsets that transport us to new domains to ordinary things like cell phones that have turned into an expansion of ourselves, item development can reshape how we live, work, and play.

Yet, innovation doesn't stop at contraptions and innovative wonders. It influences all parts of our lives, from the items we use at home to those we experience expertly. Ponder the clever plan of room saving furnishings, creating eco-accommodating bundling arrangements, or acquainting plant-based options with conventional meat items.

2. PROCESS INNOVATION

Process innovation is the execution of a new or further developed technique for creating or conveying merchandise. Organizations participate in process development to elevate creation levels, work on the nature of items, and lower creation costs. Process development involves improving or utilizing new programming, hardware, or procedures to make the whole presentation process more successful and proficient. The cycle happens when an organization tries to take care of a hierarchical issue by utilizing an alternate methodology from the standard one to make the interaction more valuable to the specialists and those ward on it.

For example, an entrepreneur with different stores of items and administrations might need to take part in process development to work on the conveyance of finance really looks at through computerized programming because of many recruited representatives. This will assist with causing the interaction by which workers to accept their checks run all the more easily.

Process innovation is gainful to an association in the accompanying ways:

Expanding efficiency - Cycle development increases efficiency by laying out new cycles and further developing existing ones that bring down the time utilized and produce more wares inside a short time period. Upgrading productivity in strategic approaches - The improvement of cycles and the foundation of new frameworks make activities more sensible and more proficient by presenting new procedures and innovation that makes work simpler, frequently by freeing representatives from manual work that takes more time and squanders assets. Innovation can diminish desk work and brings down the utilization of assets. Diminishing expenses - Cycle advancement brings down costs that might be utilized while recruiting more representatives. New frameworks and innovation lessen the requirement for manual work by representatives, diminishing the utilization of numerous assets and the cash for paying workers.

3. ORGANIZATIONAL INNOVATION

Organizational innovation alludes to the improvement of another hierarchical and an organizational system that will in some way or another change an organization's strategic policies, as well as how its working environment is coordinated and its relationship with outside partners. It also connects with underlying or procedural changes inside the organization, enveloping changes in administration rehearses, working environment culture, representative commitment, and human asset methodologies.

4. MARKETING INNOVATION

Marketing innovation is the joining of new advertising strategies and procedures that contrast from the past ones and include huge changes in item advancement, plan, bundling, and arrangement. It works on an item or administration and contact a more extensive crowd. Innovation in marketing isn't just the consolidation of new innovation yet in addition the execution of new compelling thoughts. Development is fundamental since it works on your item or administration. With advancement, you can arrive at new business sectors, and increment deals and income.

Innovation can be introduced in various structures and impact different region of a business. You can bring new innovations or thoughts into training with the goal that your organization can bear outing from the opposition. Subsequent to executing a few changes, you could see higher consumer loyalty, more deals, and higher benefit. Consider carrying out plan, assembling, and item development relying upon your necessities and issues.

Assuming you figure out how to adjust to buyer inclinations, requirements, and conduct, you can zero in on your clients. Creative promoting procedures and missions empower you to track down the right way to deal with your ideal interest group and win their consideration. Lead exploration to figure out the highlights your item needs for a superior client experience. Fantastic client experience will carry advantages to your clients and business as a business leader.

PART OF INNOVATION IN GAINING A COMPETITIVE EDGE

Innovation is one of the keys to developing your business and expanding its competitiveness. It can help you with working on your effectiveness, drop costs, and become more productive. Since little to medium- sized associations generally are not as equipped for profit from husbandry of scale as huge associations would be suitable to, the capacity to advance turns out to be much more significant. Innovation can not and ought not bere-appropriated. All effects being equal, it ought to begin inside your association. Little or average- sized associations constantly advance by rolling out little advancements to work on their tasks. It wouldn't feel OK to involve a reconsidered association for the gig, as moving the adventure takes a great deal of time nonetheless needs help. Likewise, because it's not monetarily practical for further modest associations to buy invention through accessions, making it a piece of regular work is stupendous and the most expense- complete choice. These are six(6) abecedarian places of innovation in gaining a competitive edge.

1. Market Distinction

Innovative products or administrations put a business away from contenders, drawing in guests looking for extraordinary and predominant benefactions.

2. Upgraded Productivity and Cost-Viability

Process inventions smooth out conditioning, lessen costs, and further develop effectiveness, taking into account Machiavellian estimating and further developed edges.

3. Consumer fidelity and Unwaveringly

Innovation arrangements that address customer requirements and trouble spots successfully encourage customer trustability and creation, adding to a strong customer base.

4. Versatility to Changing Business sector Requests

inventions guarantee an association can snappily answer shifts in purchaser inclinations, arising advances, or request patterns, keeping up with the significance and piece of the pie.

5. Threat Relief and Strength

Businesses that embrace inventions are more positioned to explore troubles, disturbances, and vulnerabilities, making them stronger in advancing business sectors.

6. Fascination and Maintenance of Ability:

A culture of innovations draws in top ability looking for potential open doors for development, learning, and adding to state of the art projects.

All in all, Innovation is a diverse idea enveloping product, process, organizational , and marketing innovations. Its part in acquiring an upper hand couldn't possibly be more significant, as it engages organizations to separate themselves, adjust to showcase elements, upgrade proficiency, and eventually flourish in an exceptionally cutthroat business scene.

INNOVATION STRATEGIES FOR BUSINESS SUCCESS

Innovation strategies for business success frequently include encouraging a culture of imagination, putting resources into innovative work, remaining informed about industry patterns, teaming up with outer accomplices, and being available to testing and repeating on thoughts. It's pivotal to adjust development endeavors to business objectives, focus on client needs, and influence arising innovations to acquire an upper hand. Furthermore, uplifting cross-useful cooperation and giving a steady climate to risk-taking can spike creative reasoning inside an association. There are open innovations, design thinking or reasoning, and Dexterous techniques.

● **Open innovation:**

Teaming up with outer accomplices, clients, and contenders to encourage innovation and drive development includes drawing in with partners past the limits of an organization. It's tied in with pooling assorted points of view, mastery, and assets to make novel thoughts, items, or administrations that benefit every elaborate party. This cooperation can prompt shared experiences, quicker improvement, decreased costs, and upgraded market reach. By utilizing each other's assets, associations can remain cutthroat and drive development in an undeniably interconnected and dynamic business climate.

● **Design Thinking:**

Design thinking is a human-driven approach that includes understanding and sympathizing with clients to make arrangements that address their necessities and inclinations. By putting the client at the center of the plan cycle, organizations can acquire significant experiences into their main interest group.

This client-driven center aides in creating items or administrations that truly resound with clients, prompting expanded fulfillment and unwaveringly. Understanding their trouble spots and wants takes into consideration the advancement of additional important and successful arrangements.

Moreover, design thinking supports imaginative reasoning by advancing inventiveness and coordinated effort. It encourages a climate where various viewpoints and thoughts are invited, prompting out-of-the-container arrangements that can separate a business on the lookout.

As far as business execution, the iterative idea of design thinking empowers speedy prototyping and testing, decreasing the gamble of concentrating intently on thoughts that may not work. This dexterity improves proficiency and cost-adequacy, at last decidedly affecting the main concern.

● **Dexterous Techniques:**

Dexterous techniques advance iterative turn of events, taking into consideration incessant criticism and changes, prompting a more refined and proficient finished result. They upgrade flexibility by empowering groups to answer quickly to changes in necessities, innovation, or economic situations, guaranteeing the item remains lined up with partners' requirements. Spry cultivates straightforwardness, cooperation, and client inclusion, upgrading item quality and consumer loyalty through a persistent criticism circle. Furthermore, it supports an adaptable workplace, enabling groups to self-sort out and focus on undertakings, at last upgrading projects, the board and conveyance.

In all of this chapter, simply understand that, Innovations hold tremendous potential for organizations, both in substantial additions like expanded productivity and income, and theoretical advantages like upgraded brand notoriety and representative resolve. Embracing a culture of development empowers inventive reasoning and critical thinking, cultivating an upper hand. Utilizing arising advancements takes into account smoothed out processes and new market open doors. By taking on imaginative systems, organizations can adjust, develop, and thrive in the present exceptionally cutthroat business climate. You need to embrace innovations based on your set goals of your businesses to unlock the dimension of wealth you want to accumulate.

CHAPTER 9

BUSINESS GROWTH AND EXPANSION

In this final chapter, we dig into the basic parts of business growth and expansion, crucial for maintaining and flourishing in the present serious market. Growth and Expansion are critical stages in an organization's life cycle, and understanding how to explore them is fundamental for long haul achievement.

● **Understanding Growth Strategies**

1. **Market Penetration:**

The Pros: Uses existing items in existing business sectors to increment piece of the pie and client base. Requires less gamble and speculation contrasted with different techniques.

The Cons: Restricted development or growth potential as it depends on existing items and markets.

When to Utilize: When the market has undiscovered portions or when you can increment deals through advancements, promoting, or further developed dispersion.

2. Market Advancement:

The Pros : Targets new business sectors or market fragments, extending the client base and income potential.

The Cons: Requires statistical surveying, variation of items or administrations, and may confront administrative or social difficulties in new business sectors.

When to Utilize: When current business sectors are soaked, or when there's a need to broaden and investigate undiscovered geographic or segment markets.

3.Product Development:

The Pros: Includes making and offering new items or administrations to existing business sectors, drawing in new clients and expanding income streams.

The Cons: Includes high examination, improvement, and promoting expenses, and there's a gamble that the new item probably won't succeed.

When to Utilize: When there's interest for creative or further developed items, or when you have the abilities to put resources into innovative work.

1. Diversification:

The Pros: Includes entering completely new business sectors with new items or administrations, spreading risk and possibly boosting returns.

The Cons: High gamble because of absence of involvement with the new market and likely redirection of assets from existing effective regions.

When to Utilize: When the ongoing business sector is immersed or declining, and there are open doors for development in irrelevant business sectors.

STRATEGIC CASE STUDIES AND UNIQUE PRACTICES

I'm presenting this real life case studies to you as my dear reader in order to enhance your strength, discover your weaknesses, challenges, and how to go about them as you get access to these real life case study.

1. Amazon

Amazon has been my best online shopping experience. Amazon is just an amazing platform.

• Strategy: Amazon began as a web-based book shop and ventured into a worldwide online business goliath by expanding its item contributions and putting vigorously in innovation and strategies.

• Challenges: Wild rivalry, functional versatility, and overseeing client assumptions during quick development.

● Lessons: Versatility, client centricity, persistent development, and putting resources into foundation are urgent for extension.

1. Tesla:

● Strategy: Tesla started with electric vehicles and ventured into energy arrangements and independent driving innovation, zeroing in on manageability and development.

● Challenges: High capital prerequisites, mechanical progressions, administrative obstacles, and market acknowledgment.

● Lessons: Troublesome development, ecological awareness, and vital associations are keys to effective extension.

1. Uber:

● Strategy: Uber upset the transportation business by presenting a helpful ride-sharing stage through a versatile application.

● Challenges: Administrative deterrents, neighborhood contest, and driver-accomplice fulfillment and maintenance.

● Lessons: Utilizing innovation for interruption, powerful partner the executives, and understanding nearby business sectors are crucial for worldwide development.

1. Alibaba:

● Strategy : Alibaba began as a B2B web based business stage and ventured into different areas like retail, finance, distributed computing, and planned operations.

● Challenges: Exploring the complicated Chinese market, worldwide development, and laying out entrust with worldwide accomplices.

- Lessons: Expansion, grasping social subtleties, and vital acquisitions encourage practical development.

UNIQUE PRACTICES

Client Driven Approach : Comprehend and satisfy client needs.

Development and Versatility: Embrace change and advance to remain in front of the opposition.

Interest in Innovation: Influence innovation for productivity, versatility, and better client encounters.

Vital Organizations and Unions: Team up to get to new business sectors and assets.

Worldwide Market Getting it : Designer methodologies as indicated by the social, monetary, and administrative parts of explicit business sectors.

Risk The board and Adaptability : Expect difficulties and be adaptable in changing techniques as needs be.

These accepted procedures apply across enterprises and business sizes, underscoring the significance of advancement, client center, vital preparation, and flexibility in accomplishing fruitful business extensions.

CONCLUSION

In the zenith of this illuminating excursion through the domains of key development, we have uncovered the essential bits of insight that push organizations towards getting through flourishing. Through fastidious investigation and smart examination, we've enlightened the pathways to accumulating abundance while guaranteeing the sacredness of supportability. Presently, equipped with the cunning authority of technique, may you leave on your pioneering odyssey with mental fortitude, vision, and the unfaltering obligation to develop business abundance that endures the ways of the world — securely, reasonably, and brilliantly. For in the realm of vital development, the material is tremendous, the conceivable outcomes limitless, and the brushstrokes of progress never-ending. See you at the acme of life.